Dandelions

Mamta Pahuja

Writer's Pocket

First published by Writer's Pocket in 2023

email: publish@writerspocket.com

cover design by Khushi Desai

ISBN-13: 978-93-6083-520-0

www.writerspocket.com

This book is a dedication to the love in my heart, without which I would be nothing but a void in the space. It's an existence like an elixir that's my muse, music, devotion and prayer.

CONTENTS

ACKNOWLEDGMENTS

Thank you is a small word for so many, who believed in my pursuit and encouraged me. Most of my friends are people from virtual world, but they have read my work for years and have supported me in finding my dream. Many a people from across border have practically held my hand through this journey and are as joyous as I am seeing my work in print.
A sincere thanks and appreciation for being a part of my journey.

1. My dreams

If only…
I could run my fingers through my dreams
I would touch them with a reverence…
a delicacy…
Of touching a dandelion…
I would protect them
From the winds of time
And whisper to them love
For they have you in them.

2. Spring in me

My memories carry fragrance of you
Every night…
You bloom in me as I sit there
mesmerised
Watching every petal open gently
Touching all my senses…
I let myself drown in the sensations of you
As if…slow death seeping into my veins
This poison…sweeter than saccharine
Seeps into my bones …
Until, I fall asleep

And at the twilight
I open my eyes…
Scared… to find you gone again
The spring in me passes…
I spend the day among the dead leaves
Waiting for the season to turn again
For the fragrance of you
To come to life
The array continues…
The dream lives on
Waiting for the hope to die.

3. Goodbye

Smell of yellow pages
Reviving some old memories
Rain falling through my eyes
The fog on the old stained glass
Misting my thoughts
The empty coffee shop
Is finally a solace to heart…
That wants to feel the solitude
And
Unmute some of my silent cries
So it can let go of those
Who left without so much as a goodbye
It's finally time to bid them to memories….
and cry.

4. If I were an artist

I just figured…
If I were an artist…
I could draw you
Everywhere
I go…
All the places…
I would want to go
Holding your hand.

I could fill the spaces…
Just as you fill my mind
In all the hues…
In the varied moods
With eyes sometimes settled on a single leaf…
Like a wonder…
And at other times…
Wandering… as if trying to find…
Where you would like to settle your fingers…

I would paint the pictures of you
On the walls
And fill my home
With your dimpled smile…
And then…
Perhaps, I would sleep in peace
Knowing you are all around
Even when, you are miles away…

Only, if I were an artist…

5. I shall wait

Across the lifetimes…
Is a meadow
Where, I shall wait
Among a burst of colours
Or the grey stones of cemeteries
In the stillness of water
Or a gale
I shall wait…
Until…you arrive
And decide to stay.

6. Memories

Sitting under the twilight
With my eyes closed
Trying to draw comfort in the last moments of night…
Before the dawn breaks
I accidentally opened the casket
That I had buried long ago
In the deepest depths of my heart…
And now I have my hands full
With the memories
That I have refused myself to delve into
And now…
They are tumbling out
Furiously…
With an immensity
Of a storm…
That I can't seem to stop…
Some of them are so sweet
And full of colour
Like sugar candies ready to melt in mouth…
And there are a few…
That have faded and need a bit of light
I see here, a few pages
That I had saved
From some old favourite poems
The verses are reminder of an old love
Which left…
For the want of new horizons
But, I see now I too have moved on
From some of these memories

That I no longer need to put them back in the box
I will let them go free
Below the stars…
Before the light comes
There are a precious few…
I would like to dust and sun
Before putting them back
Perhaps, not in a casket this time
But under the ground
Where they would grow as flowers
And would spread joy
Like the dandelions feathers
And a few might fall on my grave someday
As the remains of an unknown love…
Yet everlasting…
Memories… before they finally fade…

7. In between pages

Everything I write
And everything I delete
Are all enfolded in one name
That's love… that's prayer
And my muse…
More than worship
And less than death…

8. A prayer

Come back to me…
Are the only words
That I hold inside me
Every moment of each day
For saying it loud
Would taint a prayer…

9. The resilient heart

O! Poor heart
Why are you… borne of such resilience
to be tested again and again…
against the winds of change and war…
to be broken into a million pieces…
a million times
Yet…you falter and learn to love again… and again…
to what end…

10. Those eyes

I have closed my eyes
For there's nothing I would rather look at
after this day…
Having seen those eyes…
The pain of love
The torment of separation
The dream of togetherness
All so subtly contained…
Yet
Pronounced…
Like the morning scream for a coffee
When I open my eyes
All I desire is
to look into those eyes…
And drink from them.

11. God or creation of God

…and I kissed those feet
For the journey he made
From heaven to earth
To uplift… to love…
He is the bringer of peace
But… I have seen him dwell
In something
Deep…
deeper… than the ocean
The demeanour was calm
The eyes…
Hauntingly beautiful …
With a touch of green
I drowned several times
too deep… to emerge again
The emotions… as if liquid
A rawness beyond years
The need… contained
Yet… love… unfastened
Between the moments
of despair and delight
The moments of weakness
so perfectly woven in strength
I wonder…
God… or the creation of God

12. You are love

I don't look for you… anymore
Don't even try to feel you
It would be like
betraying you
To try to find you
anywhere outside of myself
You are my eternal… eternity
Breath and fire
That keeps me
rooted
In light… in darkness
In faith and in doubt…
You are love.

13. I exist in another dimension

And I agreed…
To let love lead my soul
It's a sense of being senseless somedays…
like a private invitation to the pain
And on the others…
It's a sense of liberation
the knowledge…
of an existence
beyond a physicality…
Knowing, even if I am a passing thought
In someone's heart
I exist in another dimension
A universe…
where I am not there…
Yet, a speck of me appeared
Like a light
Or a shooting star
Before it went dark.
I existed… or shall I say
Exist.

14. Ohh! The pain

I felt it in great measures…
And it kept returning
Afresh…
No matter what I did to keep it at bay
Then one day… I accepted
It as my friend
Now… we almost live in harmony
Keeping each other company…
Reminding… we are just around the corner
Yes…
It's pain
The pain… that keeps returning
As a reminder…
I am alive
And in love…
With pain…And more.

15. I burn

And he set me on fire
To burn till eternity…
Now… I burn
In my own desires
After burning
the soul
that was my home…

16. Will you fall in love again!

Maybe…
You will fall in love with me
All over again…
If only…
You would close your eyes
And allow me to walk through the door
Another day of holding
one another
on a lazy day…
Cups of tea and coffee
Before we could drink through
Each other's eyes…
While the glasses clink…

Maybe…
You will fall in love with me
All over again…
And the madness would run its course again.

17. My death certificate

…and in that moment
My death certificate was signed
I watched in awe…
And wondered...
Is it ritualistic to cry
But the tears had abandoned me
They were somewhere distant
Laughing at my agony
I stood there…
Feeling the pain in my chest
Coursing through my veins
A thousand needles
Pricking…
For love had averted his eyes.
And then
My death certificate was signed
again and again
A thousand times over…
Until… I finally died
This time… at the hands of death
And it freed me
Of watching
My death certificate being signed.

18. Salvation

Every thought of you is a prayer
Every prayer has you in it
I don't know…
It's love or worship
I don't even understand
It's a wish or a hope
But it's my salvation…
The only way
I know to live
And find liberation…

19. Your silence

I have often thought
What death would look like…
I sit by my window
Unseeing….
In the infinite darkness
That stretches till the eye can see
I hear the shadows cross over
And it all feels like life…
So alive…
Twinkling amidst the little lights
And then there are days…
When you go quiet
And the light inside me dies…
Yes…that's what must be the death…
Your silence…
The world inside me stops ticking
The shadows stop midway…
As if waiting for a cue
For someone to hold their hand
Or call out…
Just a little word…
That will make them feel
Their existence is not hollow
They are owned by their beings…
That breathe life in them
But it's your silence…
That pierces my soul
And I know…
That's the call of death…

Not in a robe
Not surrounded by darkness…
Just a soul stirring quiet…
Yes… your silence is death of me.

20. A half name on my lips

A last taken breath
With a half name on my lips…
like a last prayer
The soul has taken its flight
The bearer of the coffin
In a hurry to lay the remains to rest
A few flowers that will wither in a day…
Leaving the stench of stale death

All that would remain
And would be carried across the oceans
Will be a prayer…
The half name
On my lips…
A remnant of love…
The last of me
In the quiet whispers of breeze
For a moment…

And then…a wisp of smoke
In the thin air.

21. A forgotten dream

It's like the wisp of smoke
You appear in my dreamscape
And as I stretch my wings
To take a flight
To catch the wind
The smoke dissipates...
All that remains is a thought...
An outline of a face
That I know...
From a far away land of snow
I close my eyes
To see you again...
To exchange a kiss
To touch your face
To hear your gentle voice
Or your heartbeat....
But like a wisp of smoke
You disband...
Disappear
I open my eyes...
And picture you
Holding a cup of tea
Deep in contemplation of life
Or love...
I know not
But...I know...
You are there....somewhere....
Sometimes, I too appear on your horizon...
As an outline...

Or a wisp of smoke…
And then perhaps
You close your eyes to my existence…
And I dissipate and disband
A forgotten dream
Or a nightmare.

22. Birdie

Do I want a name with the 'wings'
Yes… so I could fly like a little bird
And go round and round in the gardens of beloved…
I could stay perched on a window all night
Just to gaze at him sleeping…
And wake up at the first rays of sunshine…
To call his name
In my bird song…

Yes…I want a name with the wings…
Even if it's called a little 'birdie'
That my fellows would laugh at…
But I would have my secret power to fly
Perhaps, only in my dreams

But, I like to think…
I would like a name with the 'wings'

23. Between words and silence

Between words and silence
Run my thoughts amok
There are days…
I wish I could put them on a burner
And walk away

And there are times…
When the emptiness in me gets so deep
That it drowns me
In its waves…

Between words and silence
I exist in a dimension
That's a universe in itself
With its infinite possibilities of war and peace
Where I have the power to create
And to destroy…

I am my own Goddess
In the mirror
That hangs between
The two worlds of…
Words and silence.

24. Love that I have lost

Listening to the rain drops crackle on my window…
My heart goes in shadows of past
When I used to find joy in these sprinkles…
I imagined myself holding a hand…
And walking in the cool breeze
soaked in rain…
Sitting in some small corner tea stall…
Ordering two glasses of tea with chattering teeth
And watch him drink both of them
For… I was always stubborn about my coffee…
Now… all I have left are these thoughts…
The non stop rain…
And a heart
That craves…
That feathery touch of those fingers
That always left me wanting something more…
Today… I have just closed my eyes
And the window…
Trying to not feel all the love that I have lost…

25. That name

Yes…
I say that name
To feel the sweetness on my lips…
To remember
The peace I always feel…
The presence of butterflies is still there
I can hear the flutter in my heart
And my soul takes a flight
Thousands of miles
millions of times…
To reminisce that sweet scent of snow

Yes…
I say that name
As a chant…
For it's my quintessential
In this mortal world
My deliverance from pain…
It's like a walk home
After being lost for a long time…

Yes…
I say that name.

26. Fragility of life

A night with the touch of silence…
gazing at the stars in dark sky
feeling suspended…
between the heaven and orb…
Sound of water in distance…
The sense of no longer being tied to any place…
Thoughts all quiet…
The sense of calm as deep as eternal rest…
The strangeness of being…
Fragrance of night blooms…
Rising from the graveyard…
A reminder of fragility of life...
Wondering… Is life just a moment…
To be lived in obedience…
Or feeling alive…

27. Love has returned

The arrival of fresh batch of dreams…
In the summer's blue skies…
The birds taking off early…
Chattering all the way…
As if caught in a frenzy of excitement of a new day…
The endless cups of icy coffee…
Long days of outdoor play…
Little girls flitting about in the bright sunshine…
Boys in the football field…
The evenings filled with golden glow of sunsets…
The long lazy dinners at the beach…
Filled with delicious candle lights…
The balmy breeze…
The anticipation of long nights filled with pain and
passions…
The quite bliss of the knowledge…
Love has returned…
This time to stay.

28. 20 seconds

20 seconds…
I looked into the eyes of life
And we both drowned…
In the depths of doom…
Now, life doesn't know…
Why… I have been dead so long…
And I don't know…
When I had a chance at living…
Why I chose to die.
As much as death is the eternal truth…
I figured… so is life.

29. Fireflies

…and my soul
set about to quell the darkness on a moonless night...
found a thousand fireflies
Together they danced until the darkest hour
...before the twilight

30. Would she melt

In the mind of his eye...
He saw her smiling that mellow smile...
The one knowing of all...
How in this moment... he is dying to have her...
And relish her... claiming every thought in that dainty head of hers...
Just by brushing his warm breath…
Against her neck...
And she would melt faster than a candle...
Burning at the altar.

31. Atlas

As I was reminiscing some old forgotten memories
An image swam in front of me
An image of blues browns and greens
A reproduction of a long forgotten Atlas

The two dimensional world
That existed in those pages
The enigma that they held in those days
Again caught hold of my inquisitiveness

And I decided to look for one, yet again
After an intense search
I found one yellow paged dog eared
In the bottom most drawer of my memoirs

As I began leafing through the pages
Tracing my fingers on some of those mountains and
rivers
Somewhere the thought struck
Isn't this what life is about

The highs and lows
The depression and exuberance
And gradually turning pale as the pages
Reaching the end along with the frayed edges

And one day
It will all be history.

32. Weight of words

Nothingness
Is what I wish to carry in my heart
For I am tired of love

Love...
Comes with words
Words that are often hollow
Yet the weight of them is heavier than earth.

I wish to hear silence
The one that reverberates in the rhythm of heart
That speaks volumes in its quietude.

Let me hear your silence
That doesn't lie
That knows not to betray
Let's not hide behind words today

They will again apologize
At their own afflictions
When we will both understand each other's silence
We will know

Words were mere aberrations
Over silence that could speak much louder.

33. I wish to fill these silences

Every silence in my being
Stretches like a desert
Unending storms... the sand flying everywhere
Blinding me... filling my mouth
With incomprehensible words
That I can't utter
Without swallowing the whole strand.

And then
The scorching sun
Burning me to cinders
With no respite in sight
There are mirages…
But no oases

I wish to fill these silences
With love...
With throbbing sounds of a beating heart
With a glimmer of hope
With a heart break...

Something... something, that's more tangible
Than the forever stretching time
And this Kalahari of my life
Where I go on living
Without a respite in sight.

34. She would find her light

…and the butterfly rose again
On those fragile wings
The wind was strong
But the conviction stronger...
This time, she won't let her soul drown
Let all the candles burn themselves into darkness…
She would find her light in the world beyond.

35. My wrinkled dreams

In the creases of night
I hide
My wrinkled dreams
I have collected them through life.

Some of them stolen from the ashes of time
Others, snatched from the wind
That threatened
To take them away.

A few were lying in the fog of misery
There were others
That I picked among the fallen leaves
Some I found astray in the moonlight.

And then with the twilight
I started unfolding each one of them
Carefully,
One by one.

Ensuring I don't spill them
Or lose them again
In the middle of broken paths
Or, in the remoteness of my dark thoughts.

These are the oysters that will give birth to pearls
I will string them
Until,
I have fastened each one of them in the thread of life.

36. Through love and heartaches

Today, I started folding pain...
To stack it in the shelves of life...
And put some of it away...
It has been spilling... like my wardrobe...
That has no more space left...
And, I noticed...
How much have I earned through the life...
Some of it has collected dust... over the years...
Yet, when I brought it out...
The sheen is not lost...
It has not shrunk... over the years
Pain...You are just as precious... a reminder...
Of a life lived...
Through love and heartaches...

37. It was only you

I want to write my every thought
Just for you...
So you know...
When I am no more
I was never there...
It was only you.

38. You exist in me

You move in me like an ocean...
Taking up all the space...
Filling me to the brim...
Somedays, you are quiet like deep waters…
Other days, you come roaring like high tides and leave me assailed...
Somedays, you are comfort like a cup of coffee...
On the others, leave me thinking of tea.

39. A kiss of deliverance

Two hearts bound by the burning string of love…
There's no shade
Only sun
In the desert…
The lips dried and parched
Awaiting the kiss of deliverance
The kiss may be eons away…
In between are the seas of doubts
Yet… a faith held by the soul
When the hearts taste salt
There shall be a recompense…
Before the end
A love to relive and revive…
All that's lost
In the mists of time
Finally, a kiss before the end.

40. Hope

Hope...
Why do you keep slipping in…
And break my heart yet again...
I have accepted the effete of my fate…
And now, I wish to rest my case...
We both have been together... long enough
To learn...
We don’t belong.

41. The moments

So often I meet people…
Fall in love…
For no reason…
We serve our purpose for one another...
Without looking for a personal gain
We hold hands…
Exchange our energies...
Spend a few precious moments… leave a mark for lifetime
And move on...

Carrying memories...
That fade with time…
Like those precious vases…
That broke…
Without intent...

Somedays, we sit and recollect
All those memoirs…
And they don't feel misspent…
To me they come across...
Not as a lesson or an experience...
But, the moments
That were meant to be opportunities...
For opening new doorways...
The ones I never knew existed…

42. Beloved

Beloved
You are in me so deep down
That if a teardrop falls from your eye
My soul gets drenched.
Beloved…
Somedays I wish to hold your hand
And feel your warmth against my cold skin
A touch so gentle
Featherlike…
That goes so deep down
It moves my soul.
Beloved…
It's not the mountains
that move my grit
It's not the rivers
that soak my skin
It's your love
that drowns my soul.

43. Void of unsaid

I want to write a novel about silence...
The things people don't say...
Said he.
Leaves me wondering...
How often do we hear...
The unsaid...
And if we would...
What would the world come to?
Will there be more wars?
Or the hearts will find contentment...
In all they had to internalise...
Sometimes, for the peace to continue...
On the others...
Simply, for the worthlessness of expressing...
When it falls on deaf ears...
I want to write a novel about "silence"...
The things people don't say...
Said he.
Will it be a blank page...
Or it will go on for ever and ever...
For what's left unsaid...
Fills the skies with rain...
And eyes with oceans...
Let's leave the unsaid in its silence...
And embrace the voices...
That fill the void of unsaid...

Said I.

44. Curtains within

Search not with your eyes
Close them
And you will find

It's all a part of you
Every dream
Each miracle
Lies within you

As you raise the curtains within
You will know
You are the wonder
You have been looking for

Stay
It's all in the creases of you
Unfold them

And find you.

45. My karma

Pen is my karma...
As I hold it and run across its feather tip…
It leaves some most permanent marks...
Across the pages and on my heart...
The stories it creates…
Are my essence and my fate.

ABOUT THE AUTHOR

Mamta Pahuja, is not a name yet heard by anyone yet, but she lives to love and to dream of making a space for herself in the world of poetry through her work, that she believes she will a small blot, if not a mark someday.

Writer's Pocket

Writer's Pocket is a publication house established in 2016. We began with the aim of providing a better publishing platform for aspiring writers and budding poets.

The publishing industry in India (and around the world, to a great extent) is always something of a mystery even to the writers themselves. We are working on making publishing more accessible to everyone.

So far, we have helped over 3,000 writers turn their dreams into reality by publishing the books and continue to do so. By doing so, we also provide some of the best content by Indian writers to the readers.

Want to read more books? Scan this QR code with your smartphone and check out all our books on Amazon.